American Lives

Ida B. Wells-Barnett

Heidi Moore

Heinemann Library
Chicago, Illinois

Designed by Heinemann Library
Photo research by Eva Schorr
Printed in China by WKT Company Limited.

08 07 06 05 04
10 9 8 7 6 5 4 3 2 1

Library of Congress Cataloging-in-Publication Data
Moore, Heidi, 1976-
  Ida B. Wells-Barnett / Heidi Moore.
     p. cm. -- (American lives)
Summary: A biography of Ida B. Wells-Barnett, a
former slave who became journalist dedicated to
equal rights, and who fought especially for women's
right to vote and an end to lynching.
Includes bibliographical references (p.   ) and index.
  ISBN 1-4034-4997-X (Hardcover) -- ISBN 1-4034-
5706-9 (Paperback)
 1. Wells-Barnett, Ida B., 1862-1931--Juvenile
literature. 2. African American women civil rights
workers--Biography--Juvenile literature. 3. Civil
rights workers--United States--Biography--Juvenile
literature. 4. Journalists--United States--Biography--
Juvenile literature. 5. African Americans--Civil
rights--History--Juvenile literature. 6. Lynching--
United States--History--Juvenile literature. 7.
United States--Race relations--Juvenile literature.
[1. Wells-Barnett, Ida B., 1862-1931. 2. Civil rights
workers. 3. Journalists. 4. African Americans--
Biography. 5. Women--Biography.] I. Title. II.
American lives (Heinemann Library (Firm))
E185.97.W55M66 2004
973'.0496073'0092--dc22

2003015755

Acknowledgments
The author and publishers are grateful to the
following for permission to reproduce copyright
material: Title page, pp. 4, 15, 22, 25 Library of
Congress; pp. 5, 17, 21, 23, 24, 26, 28 University
of Chicago Library; p. 6 Linda Jones/Courtesy
of The South Reporter, Holly Springs, MS; p. 7
Marshall County Historical Museum, from the
Smith Collection. P.O.B. 806, Holly Springs
Mississippi; p. 8 New York Times; pp. 9, 16 The
Granger Collection, New York; p. 10 Corbis; p. 11
LeMoyne-Owen College; p. 12 From the Collection
of the Chesapeake and Ohio Historical Society, Inc.;
pp. 13, 18 Ohio Historical Center Archives Library;
p. 20 Bettmann/Corbis; p. 27 Bob Thall for the
Chicago Landmarks Commission; p. 29 Bettmann/
Corbis

Cover photograph by University of Chicago Library

The author would like to thank her husband James
and her editor, Angela McHaney Brown.

The publisher would like to thank Michelle Rimsa
for her comments in the preparation of this book.

Every effort has been made to contact copyright
holders of any material reproduced in this book.
Any omissions will be rectified in subsequent
printings if notice is given to the publisher.

The cover image of Ida B. Wells-Barnett was taken in
1893. She was 31 years old.

Contents

Some words are shown in bold, **like this.** You can find out what they mean by looking in the glossary.

Born into Slavery

Ida Bell Wells was born in the United States on July 16, 1862. She was born a slave.

Just six months later, President Abraham Lincoln would sign the **Emancipation** Proclamation. Signing that piece of paper on January 1, 1863, was an effort to free the slaves in the South.

This is the first page of the Emancipation Proclamation that Lincoln signed.

This is a picture of Ida B. Wells-Barnett in 1893. She was 31 years old.

Ida spent her life fighting for the rights of African Americans. She was a strong and courageous woman. As a writer, she used her pen as a tool to fight for **equality.**

Ida B. Wells-Barnett believed in equal rights for African Americans and for women. She became a leader in the movement against **lynching,** which was a type of violence toward African Americans. She also joined the movement for **suffrage,** or the right to vote, for women.

Childhood

Ida grew up in Holly Springs, Mississippi. Her parents, James Wells and Elizabeth Warrenton Wells, were slaves.

Ida was born during the Civil War. Some of the southern states wanted to keep slavery, so they tried to become a separate country. That caused a war. In 1865, when Ida was three years old, the war ended. The Thirteenth **Amendment** was passed, which changed the Constitution and ended slavery in the South. Ida's parents were freed.

The house in Holly Springs where Ida was born is now a museum.

The Life of Ida B. Wells-Barnett

1862	1883	1884	1889
Born on July 16 in Holly Springs, Mississippi	*Moved to Memphis, Tennessee*	*Thrown off train and sued railroad company; Started writing articles using name Iola*	*Elected secreta of National Pr Association*

After **emancipation,** Ida's father, a carpenter, became involved in politics. Her mother worked as a cook.

Ida was the oldest child in her family. She had four younger brothers and three younger sisters. She was curious and loved to read. She read all the books in her Sunday school library.

Ida went to a school like this one in Holly Springs.

1893	1895	1913–1916	1931
Moved to Chicago, Illinois	*Published a book on lynching*	*Served as officer of the Chicago court*	*Died on March 25 in Chicago*

Yellow Fever

Ida's parents believed in the importance of education. As a teenager, Ida studied at Rust University in Holly Springs. She was a good student and loved learning.

In 1878, a yellow fever **epidemic** hit Mississippi. Luckily, Ida was away at her grandmother's farm at the time. Ida's parents and her younger brother Stanley died from the disease.

This January 1879 article from the *New York Times* talks about the yellow fever epidemic of 1878. Thousands of people had died from the disease.

THE YELLOW FEVER PLAGUE

REPORT OF THE BOARD OF EXPERTS.

STATISTICS OF THE RECENT SCOURGE—A THOROUGH STUDY OF THE DISEASE BY A MEDICAL BOARD URGED—A NATIONAL HEALTH BOARD AND A MORE PERFECT QUARANTINE SYSTEM RECOMMENDED.

WASHINGTON, Jan. 30.—The Board of Experts authorized by Congress to investigate the yellow fever epidemic of 1878 submitted their report to the Joint Congressional Committee at its meeting this morning. After quoting the several questions which were laid before them by the Joint Committee, upon which they were to base their inquiries, the report sets forth that a great number of facts have been gathered respecting the history of the late epidemic of yellow fever, which have guided the board in arriving at the conclusions which are respectfully submitted in reply to questions of the Congressional Committees on Epidemic Diseases. It should be borne in mind that these conclusions are based upon evidence of a necessarily incomplete investigation of the epidemic—incomplete, because of the urgent demand for public health legislation during the present session of Congress. Otherwise, the board might not be held excusable for the seeming haste in dealing with this great subject. The board are unanimous in the opinion that the investigation of the late epidemic should be completed, and the study of the natural history of yellow fever seonld be systematically pursued, and especially that the inquiries should embrace the perpetually infected ports of the West Indies, whose fields give the greatest promise of practical results as the reward of faithful scientific inquiry. It is accordingly recommended that two or three skilled experts be charged with the completion of the study of the late epidemic, which can be concluded in a few months, and that at least two such experts be authorized to proceed to the West Indies, there to make a more thorough study of yellow fever than has ever yet been undertaken, and that they be accompanied by an experienced microscopist. It is further recommended that the necessary steps be taken by Congress to secure the co-operation of the Spanish and other foreign Governments, through an international commission or otherwise, in an earnest effort to ascertain the cause or causes which perpetuate yellow fever from year to year in the West India Islands, and to devise ways to remove the cause or causes or to lessen the chances of transporting the poison to the United States or other countries.

To no other great nation of the earth is yellow fever so calamitous as to the United States of America. In a single season, more than 100,000 of our people were stricken in their homes, and 20,000 lives sacrificed by this preventable disease.

A SYSTEM OF QUARANTINE.

Ida taught at a schoolhouse like this one.

Ida quit school to take care of her remaining brothers and sisters. She needed to earn a living to support the family. So she took an exam to become a country schoolteacher.

Ida became a teacher at age sixteen. She made only $25 a month, which would be like making about $450 per month today.

In her own words:

"I came home every Friday afternoon, riding the six miles on the back of a big mule. I spent Saturday and Sunday washing and ironing and cooking for the children and went back to my country school on Sunday afternoon."

Learning and Teaching

Around 1883, Ida and her brothers moved to Memphis, Tennessee. Her younger sisters went to live with their Aunt Fannie. Ida took a job teaching school in the nearby town of Woodstock.

During summer vacations, she continued her studies at schools in Memphis. By 1884 she was able to teach in city schools. As a teacher, she lived in different **boarding houses** around Memphis.

This illustration shows how Memphis looked around the time Ida lived there.

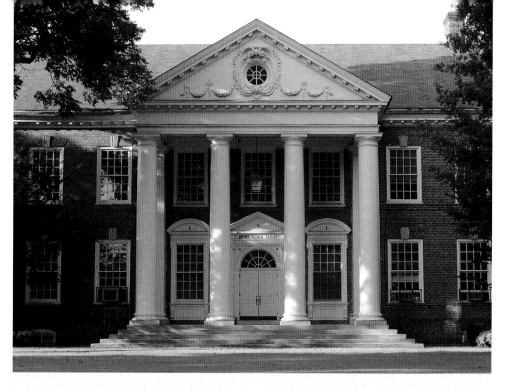

Ida went to the LeMoyne Institute, pictured above.
The school is now called LeMoyne-Owen College.

The schools where Ida taught were for
African Americans only. That was because
of **segregation.**

After the end of the Civil War, there were
still many unfair laws. Some of these laws
kept black people and white people separate
in public places like schools and train cars.

Unfair Treatment

Something happened in 1884 that would change Ida's life. She was riding in a first-class ladies' car on the Chesapeake, Ohio, and Southwestern Railroad. The conductor told her to move to the smoking car, where the other African-American passengers were sitting. She refused to give up her seat, and the conductor forced her to get off the train.

Ida was furious. She believed she should have the same right as anyone to a comfortable seat on a train. She sued the railroad company. The court first ruled in her favor, but then sided with the railroad company.

Trains during Ida's lifetime looked like the one shown here.

She started writing articles for newspapers around the country. Using the **pen name** Iola, she wrote about **discrimination,** or unfair treatment, toward women and African Americans. She used a different name so she could speak her mind without fear of facing angry readers.

When Ida's real name was later revealed, some people praised her for her powerful articles.

"IOLA" WELLS.

An Interesting Biographical Sketch—A Forcible Writer.

One of the brightest geniuses of the rising generation of women is Miss Ida B. Wells, who is well known among race journalists as "Iola." Miss Wells is a school teacher by profession, and has experienced a most eventful life. She is the eldest of eight children. She had just entered the portals of Shaw (now Rust) University, in 1878, with a view of completing her education, when the yellow fever broke out in her native town, and within twenty-four hours deprived her of her mother and father. Thus her tide of fortune ebbed ere it reached its promising flood, and she, at the tender age of sixteen, was compelled to leave the college and labor to provide for her five younger sisters and brothers who escaped the deadly disease. In that year she began her career as a school teacher, which she still continues, having a school in Memphis. In 1883 Miss Wells attempted to ride in a passenger car, and was forcibly ejected by three rough white men. She began a civil suit for damage under the State laws. In every court she got a suit for damages, except the Supreme Court, which reversed the decisions of the lower courts, causing her to lose her case. This inspired her to write an article, which she sent to a journal published by one of the race. The article created a widespread sensation, and placed her in demand as a writer. She grasped the opportunity, and is now doing good work on several journals. She is a terse and forcible writer, and plunges into politics and other matters of national importance with the vivacity of a full-fledged journalist of the masculine gender. Recently she purchased a one-third interest in the "Free Speech and Headlight," of Memphis, Tenn. She is upon its editorial staff. While the portrait we give is a good one, it hardly does Miss Wells justice. She is also secretary of the National (colored) Press Association, defeating John Wesley Cromwell, editor of the Washington, D. C., People's Advocate, who was also a candidate for the position.

IDA B. WELLS.

Princess of the Press

When she was 24, Wells traveled across the country to visit her aunt in California. She stayed there for a while and taught in a one-room schoolhouse. It was a **segregated** school, and there were not enough supplies for all the students.

In 1887, she decided to return to Memphis to teach. She started writing for African-American newspapers, including the *Free Speech and Headlight*. She also became secretary of the National Press Association.

Heading west

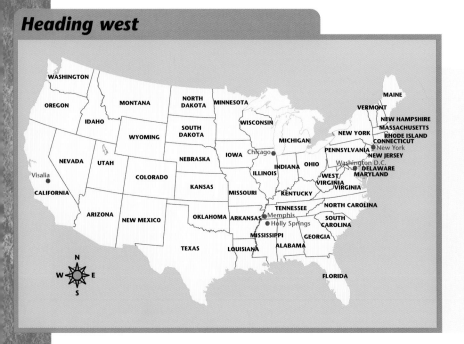

In 1886 Ida traveled west by train through Missouri, Kansas, Colorado, Utah, and Nevada to California.

In 1889, Ida took the money she had earned from writing and teaching and bought one-third of the *Free Speech and Headlight*. As the paper's editor, she wrote about the problems in the Memphis school system. The people who ran the school were upset about the articles. In 1891, the Memphis **School Board,** a group in charge of all the schools in Memphis, fired her.

Nickname

African-American editors gave Ida B. Wells the nickname "Princess of the Press." At the time, there were few women journalists.

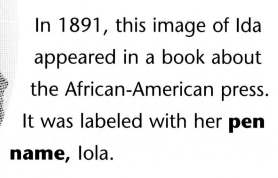

In 1891, this image of Ida appeared in a book about the African-American press. It was labeled with her **pen name,** Iola.

Violence and Anger

Soon African-American newspapers all over the country were printing Ida's articles. She had become a well-known **journalist.**

Ida used her newspaper articles to speak out against **discrimination.** She often wrote about the unfair treatment of women and African Americans. Some people did not agree with her, but many others shared her beliefs about **equality.**

This illustration shows an African-American man being asked to leave a train car. Ida did not believe **segregation** like this was fair.

Ida is shown here (on the right) with the widow of Tom Moss, one of the men lynched in Memphis.

Another event changed her life in 1892. Three of her friends were **lynched,** or violently attacked by a **mob.**

Ida was very upset. She started writing articles calling for an end to violence against innocent people based solely on race.

Power of the Pen

In one article, Ida asked people living in Memphis to **boycott,** or not use, the streetcars. She believed the people who ran the streetcar company had been involved in **lynchings** of African Americans. She also wrote other articles focused on **discrimination** and violence against African Americans.

Her articles angered many white Americans. An angry **mob** broke into her office at the *Free Speech.* Luckily she was not there, so she was not hurt. The mob trashed her office and broke her things.

This is a newspaper column Ida wrote after her office was destroyed.

IDA B. WELL

Her Reply to Gov. No
and Others.

THE LYNCHING REC

Effect in England of A
by Memphis Papers

The English Papers and
Resent the Attack on
Miss Wells.

LONDON, Eng., June 23.—The
weeks' agitation in this city
lynch law has waked up the sou
sides Gov. Northen's letter of
denial and request that the
people get their facts from a '
ble' source, the southern pr
been very active along the sam
The Memphis Daily Commer
ceeds them all in the vigor, v
and vileness of its attack, no
lynching, but upon me persona
its issue of May 26 it devoted
four columns to traduction of
sonal character, in language m
gar and obscene than anything
lice Gazette ever contained, and
up all by giving space for the fi
in its history, to an interview
colored man, J. Thomas Turn
claimed that "the respectable
population of Menphis utterly re
Ida Wells and her statements

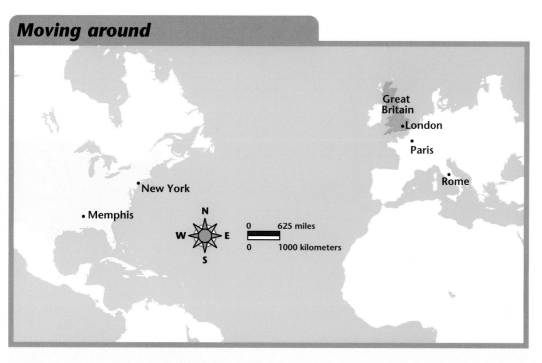

In 1893 Ida traveled by ship to speak in Great Britain about the lynching problem in the United States.

Ida had become a powerful voice in Memphis, and some people did not want to hear what she was saying. Her life was in danger. So she decided to move to New York.

In New York, Ida wrote for the *New York Age* newspaper. She also started traveling around the country to speak about lynching in the South.

Taking Action

When she returned from Europe, Ida went to Chicago. The city was having a public fair called the World's Columbian Exposition. It was to celebrate 400 years after Christopher Columbus came to North America.

Ida found out that African Americans were not allowed to take part in the Columbian Exposition. Angry, she teamed up with famous **abolitionist** Frederick Douglass and a lawyer and editor named Ferdinand Lee Barnett. Together, the three wrote a **pamphlet** that talked about **segregation** at the fair. They handed this out to people who were going to the fair.

This shows the World's Columbian Exposition in Chicago in 1893.

This picture of Ferdinand Barnett was taken about twelve years after he and Ida married.

In 1893 Ida started the Women's Era Club. It was the first club for African-American women and was later renamed the Ida B. Wells Club. Other Ida B. Wells Clubs were started all over the country.

In June 1895, at age 33, Ida married Ferdinand Barnett. She changed her name to Ida B. Wells-Barnett. She continued writing for newspapers. She bought her husband's paper, the *Chicago Conservator,* and started writing articles for it. She also became the editor of the paper.

Life in Chicago

In 1895, Wells-Barnett published a booklet called *A Red Record*. It was the first book about **lynching** in the country.

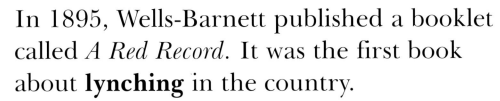

Lynch Law in Georgia.

BY

IDA B. WELLS-BARNETT

A Six-Weeks' Record in the Center of Southern Civilization, As Faithfully Chronicled by the "Atlanta Journal" and the "Atlanta Constitution."

ALSO THE FULL REPORT OF LOUIS P. LE VIN,

The Chicago Detective Sent to Investigate the Burning of Samuel Hose, the Torture and Hanging of Elijah Strickland, the Colored Preacher, and the Lynching of Nine Men for Alleged Arson.

This Pamphlet is Circulated by Chicago Colored Citizens. 2939 Princeton Avenue, Chicago.

The next year, she gave birth to a son, whom she and her husband named Charles. She kept writing articles after her son was born, and took him with her when she went on speaking tours.

This pamphlet by Ida talks about lynching in Georgia.

In 1896, Wells-Barnett traveled to Washington, D.C. She became one of the founders of the National Association of Colored Women.

She continued to speak out in public against lynching until the birth of her second son, Herman. At that point, she took time out to raise her children. She already had two young sons and would later have two daughters, as well.

Wells-Barnett is pictured here with her four children in 1909.

Working for equal rights

The National Association of Colored Women worked for job training, equal pay for men and women, child care, and education.

23

Working for Suffrage

Wells-Barnett was too busy raising children to continue being a **journalist.** But she still believed in equal rights for African Americans and women.

In the early 1900s, women did not have the right to vote. Wells-Barnett was angry about this **discrimination** against women. She started working for **suffrage,** or the right to vote, for women.

Wells-Barnett wanted things to be better for her daughters Ida (left) and Alfreda.

This suffrage parade took place in New York City on May 6, 1912. Both black women and white women marched in the parade.

Wells-Barnett was active in many African-American women's groups in Chicago. She started a group called the Alpha Suffrage Club. She served as its leader. The Alpha Suffrage Club was the first black women's suffrage group in the country.

Wells-Barnett worked with other leaders in the suffrage movement, such as Susan B. Anthony. White women and black women were now working together toward a shared goal—the right to vote.

Later Life

Wells-Barnett (second from right in middle row) shown with her husband, children, and grandchildren in 1917.

Wells-Barnett continued working to end **discrimination.** She was active in Chicago causes and a leader in the national African-American community.

In 1909 she attended a meeting that led to the National Association for the Advancement of Colored People (NAACP), a group that is still active today. Wells-Barnett also founded and became president of a group that helped African Americans moving to Chicago from the South.

Wells-Barnett and her husband lived in this house in Chicago from 1919 to 1930.

From 1913 to 1916, Wells-Barnett was an officer of the Chicago court. She even ran for the Illinois State Senate in 1930, but she did not win. At the time, there were very few African-American women in politics.

In her own words:

"I am only a mouthpiece through which to tell the story of lynching and I have told it so often that I know it by heart."

Remembering Wells-Barnett

The U.S. Postal Service printed a stamp in honor of Ida B. Wells-Barnett in 1990. This photo of her is from around 1917.

The Nineteenth **Amendment** gave women the right to vote in 1920. Without the work of Wells-Barnett, the long battle may have taken even longer. She united the suffrage movement, helping women work together for the vote.

Ida B. Wells-Barnett died in Chicago on March 25, 1931. She was 68 years old.

Wells-Barnett did not see an end to **segregation** in her lifetime. But her articles and speeches were an important part of the fight for equal rights. She also paved the way for the Civil Rights movement of the 1950s and 1960s that worked toward **equality** for African Americans.

This Civil Rights march took place in Washington, D.C., in 1963.

Wells-Barnett was a courageous woman and an important American. Born into slavery, she became a powerful **journalist** and a leader working for change. Throughout her life, she never stopped working for what she believed in.

Glossary

abolitionist person who worked to end slavery

amendment change or addition to a law or rule

boarding house house where someone rents a room and is given meals

boycott refuse to use, or buy goods from, a business or service, such as a train or a store

constitution laws of the land

discrimination unfair treatment of a person or group

emancipation freedom

epidemic disease that spreads quickly to a large number of people

equality belief that all people should have the same rights

journalist person who writes for a newspaper or magazine

lynching illegal hanging of someone by a large group

mob large group of people who break the law

pamphlet booklet

pen name fake name used when writing

school board group in charge of all the schools in an area

segregation keeping people of different races separate from each other

suffrage right to vote

More Books to Read

Keller, Kristin Thoennes. *The Women Suffrage Movement, 1848–1920.* Mankato, Minn.: Bridgestone, 2003.

McKissack, Patricia and Fredrick. *Ida B. Wells-Barnett.* Berkeley Heights, N.J.: Enslow, 2001.

Pascoe, Elaine. *The Right to Vote.* Brooklyn, N.Y.: Millbrook Press, 1997.

Places to Visit

Ida B. Wells-Barnett House
3624 S. Martin Luther King Jr., Drive
Chicago, Illinois

Ida B. Wells Art Gallery and Museum
Gatewood-Bolling Plantation
Holly Springs, Mississippi

Index